QUICK TIPS FROM THE

CBS
GOLF
SPOT

QUICK TIPS FROM THE

CBS GOLF SPOT

by Nick Seitz
Editor, Golf Digest

A
GOLF
DIGEST
BOOK

Published by Golf Digest/Tennis Inc.,
A New York Times Company
495 Westport Avenue
P.O. Box 5350
Norwalk, Connecticut 06856

Trade book distribution by
Simon and Schuster
A Division of Gulf + Western Industries, Inc.
New York, New York 10020

First Printing
ISBN: 0-914178-43-1
Library of Congress: 80-84950
Manufactured in the
United States of America

Cover and book design by Dorothy Geiser.
Typesetting by J&J Typesetters, Inc.
Norwalk, Connecticut
Printing and binding by
R.R. Donnelley & Sons

For Velma Jean, Brad and Greg—
good listeners and good critics,
considering they prefer ice hockey

TABLE OF CONTENTS

INTRODUCTION

James R. Hand, the amiably erudite chairman of the United States Golf Association's championship committee, which determines such historic matters as where the National Open will be played half a generation hence, is himself a fine senior amateur player. One morning last summer he was driving in his car to the venerable Garden City Golf Club on Long Island, where he had attained the senior final of the Walter J. Travis Memorial Tournament.

"I turned on the radio and heard your Golf Spot on CBS," he related later. "You were talking about swing tempo and how to slow it down by taking it easy at the top. It occurred to me that my own tempo had gotten too fast, and so in my match I kept your thought in mind—and hit the ball better to win the tournament."

The greatest satisfaction in doing the Golf Spot every Saturday and Sunday for eight years, first on WCBS in New York City and later on the CBS Radio Network, has come from hearing that it helps weekend golfers play better than they did the last time out. The intention, in 75 seconds of air time, has been to make one quick, simple and hopefully memorable point that a listener can apply without confusion or delay.

Improvement, Ben Hogan once told me with a riveting gaze that sent me directly to the driving range, is the true enjoyment of golf. I drew on that same conversation with

Senior golfing rivals Doug Ford and Sam Snead with Golf Digest Editor Nick Seitz.

Hogan, the greatest practicer of them all, for a Golf Spot on how and when to practice more productively.

The fringe benefit I relish most as editor of Golf Digest, the largest golf publication in the world, is the chance to work and play with the game's leading golfers and teachers. Most of the material for the radio shows is derived from the pages of the magazine and from that experience. In one recent week, if you will excuse a bit of name dropping, I was fortunate enough to play golf on different days with Tom Watson, Bob Toski and Sam Snead. (For the first time in my 43-year-old life I won money from master gamesman Snead, and the $10 bill is in the process of being framed.)

From each of them I invariably learned something. Watson gave me a useful thought on sand play, at which he has no peer these days. Toski, the head guru of the Golf Digest Instruction Schools, offered a fresh insight into plotting strategy on par-3 holes. Snead said something I'd never heard about four-ball competition—that it's smart to pick a partner who hits approximately the same distance off the tee as you do, because the two of you will be able to work together on club selection.

I see my role, then, essentially as one of synthesizing the best thinking of the best golf minds and relating it to the average player. I'm a 12 handicapper myself, and can appreciate the problems weekend golfers face. I try never to pass along advice without first testing it and finding it workable myself.

The best instruction, I have found, is both timely and timeless. A putting tip from Jack Nicklaus after he has won a record 19th major championship is topical the following week—but if it's typical Nicklaus it also will stand up long after he and I have gone to that big golf course in the sky.

Whenever possible, I have tried to make the spots fun as well as instructive. We are dealing here, after all, with a game, a leisure pursuit—not an advanced project in computer science. Most of us have learned long ago, or should have, that we are not destined to qualify for the pro tour—and we may as well relax and gain as much pleasure and companionship from this marvelous sport as we can.

In selecting the 100 spots for this book from the hundreds that have aired, I sought to cover the widest possible spectrum of material—from the full swing to the short game to strategy to equipment to the competitive and mental aspects. I also wanted to be sure the thoughts complemented each other. Larry Sheehan, editor of the Golf Digest books division, was of energetic and witty help.

Special thanks also to Bill Davis, founder of Golf Digest, who conceived the idea of the spots in the first place; Larry Dennis and Jerry Tarde, instruction editors of the magazine; Lou Adler, formerly of WCBS, who owns one of the last of the classic caddieyard swings; Dick Brescia, Frank Miller, Dave Kurman, Ida Gianetta and Debbie Palk of the CBS Radio Network, for their ongoing professionalism and encouragement, and all of you devoted listeners who suggested this compilation and voted for your favorite programs.

I suppose my own most unforgettable Golf Spot came the day one piece of tape got mixed up with another and we heard: "I'm Doctor Steven Andrew Davis. What happens when alcohol filters into your blood stream? This is Nick Seitz, editor of Golf Digest magazine, on the CBS Radio Network in the Golf Spot . . ."

Then there was the friend who summed up my side career with CBS by saying, "I think you will go far. After all, you have the perfect face for radio."

Nick Seitz
Rowayton, Conn.
January, 1982

1. SWING REMINDERS

MAKE YOUR SWING MORE THAN SUM OF ITS PARTS

A good golf swing is greater than the sum of its parts. Euclid didn't say that, but he should have.

Too much modern golf instruction is mechanical and fragmented. We are urged to think about the knees, or the right elbow, or—yes—even the left big toe. All those aspects of the swing are important, but only if they blend into a fluid entity.

It's all right to concentrate on mechanics on the practice tee, but on the course you'd better forget everything except smoothness. After all, it takes only about two seconds to make a golf swing, and that's not long enough to put one together jigsaw-puzzle style.

Practice swinging without a ball, back and forth, back and forth. Think of the swing as one flowing motion—a unified whole, not a collection of isolated parts. Then hit the ball with that same cohesive feeling, remembering that the whole of a golf swing is greater than the sum of its parts.

FORGET 'HIT' TO FACILITATE 'SWING'

The very word "hit" is one of the biggest detriments to good golf for most of us. It implies that you throw the clubhead at the ball with your hands. You try to hit the ball too hard and lose control of your swing and the shot. It's like a baseball player who thinks only of swinging for the fences—his percentages are low.

Keeping the hit impulse subdued isn't easy, because you think you need extra force to propel the ball a long way. But a hit is nothing more than what happens when the ball gets in the way of the club. Your practice swings generally are better than your real swings because there is nothing there to hit.

One excellent way to avoid hitting too hard is to imagine there is a soap bubble down there instead of a ball. Forget using excessive force and just try to burst the bubble. Swing your arms freely, and let the hit just happen, without forcing it. Once you ingrain a swing feeling you can trust, you can turn on the power to get more distance. In the meantime, try hitting the ball with your practice swing. Better yet, forget you ever heard the word "hit."

Bob Toski

SWING REMINDERS

FEEL THE FORCE

More than anything else, the weekend golfer needs to slow down his swing. There is a time and a place for speed—the clubhead should be accelerating through the ball like an airplane taking off. But most of us speed up our swings too soon, and lose control.

Why do we swing too fast? Anxiety, usually. We're in a hurry to hit the ball hard. You should be able to feel the weight and momentum of the clubhead during the swing. Otherwise you're over the speed limit. As star teaching professional Bob Toski puts it, "Feel the force. Don't force the feel."

Once you begin to develop a better paced swing, you will feel a much easier, earlier weight shift in the lower body going forward. The downswing will be starting from the legs instead of your upper body, because the legs will have time to work. But the first step in slowing down your swing is to become aware of how fast you are swinging. Can you feel the clubhead during your swing? If not, you're going too fast.

APPLY LESS EFFORT TO HIT THE BALL WITH MORE POWER

Former Masters champion Fuzzy Zoeller was the longest driver the first year he tried the tour qualifying school, but he flunked out because of wildness off the tee. As he puts it, "I hit too many in the parking lot and the water." Having learned a lesson, he began to swing with 80 percent effort instead of a hundred, and he's been improving ever since. Now he's one of the straightest long drivers in the game. His powerful but pinpoint drive on the second sudden-death playoff hole at Augusta National set up his decisive birdie in 1979.

Most weekend players think the key to hitting big drives is to swing as hard as they can. They may connect impressively now and then, but they spray the ball and score poorly. We should take a hint from Fuzzy Zoeller, who stresses that he saves his violent swings for long driving contests. On the course, he believes in "controlled power."

His fellow pros, who know how adventuresome and thunderously strong he is, marvel at his new restraint. They appreciate fully that Fuzzy's career really took off when he began driving the ball with only 80 percent of his strength. We should do the same.

Fuzzy Zoeller

ADJUST YOUR GRIP TO STRAIGHTEN SHOTS

Look to your grip if you habitually slice or hook your golf shots. The hooker of the ball, who hits it in a right-to-left roundhouse shape, should experiment with a weaker grip. That is, turn the hands more on top of the shaft, or to the left if you're right-handed. The slicer, who hits the ball left to right, should experiment with a stronger grip—turning the hands more under the shaft.

Be aware that a grip change, small as it sounds, is perhaps the hardest improvement in the game to make. You have put your hands on the club in a certain way for so long, it seems natural. Even tour pros say they will address a shot with a new grip, but their hands then sneak back into the old, comfortable alignment. Force yourself to stick with a new grip until it feels good.

And be sure you adjust both hands, not just one. Your palms should face the same way, whether more to the left to fix a hook, or more to the right to help a slice.

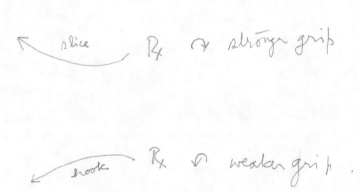

GRIP CLUB AS IF IT'S A GLASS

Tom Watson is a firm believer in light grip pressure to gain distance. If you are a typical weekend golfer, you strangle the life out of your swing. Most players grip the club so tightly they cannot possibly make a free and easy swing. Do you grip a glass tightly when you take a drink? Of course not. You shouldn't squeeze a golf club hard, either.

Watson emphasizes light grip pressure—especially in his right hand. Gripping the club lightly keeps Watson's muscles relaxed and long, so they can react faster. That means power.

A good drill for finding your correct grip pressure is to hold the club out in front of you, waist high. The minimum firmness you need to support the club is all you need to swing it.

Byron Nelson

GRIP MORE FIRMLY WITH LEFT HAND

Byron Nelson was probably the most consistent golfer ever — more recently he is known as the tutor of Tom Watson. Nelson has always advocated left-hand control as the key to consistency. He recommends that right-handers grip the club more firmly with the left hand than with the right hand. It's a lesson Watson has learned well.

With the left hand in command, you can swing the club back in a wide, disciplined arc, the left arm staying extended. And you can swing down with more leverage and control.

If the right hand and arm take over, the left arm collapses —and so does your swing arc. One common result is a weak slice.

Nelson suggests a feeling of firmness—that's firmness, not tightness—extending all the way up the left arm. That starts with your grip pressure, which again is firm in the left hand and light in the right. Then you maintain that left-hand dominance throughout the swing on all shots.

It isn't easy for a right-hander to grip more firmly with the left hand than the right, but in Byron Nelson's view, it's essential.

Raymond Floyd

USE STRAIGHT LEFT ARM AS SWING RADIUS

Bending the left arm destroys the radius of the golf swing and can cause anything from a slice to a topped shot. You should take the club back no farther than you can keep the left arm straight.

One homey cure for a collapsing left arm is to practice with a quart-size milk or juice container on your arm. Cut out the two ends of the paper carton and slip it up over your elbow. Make enough swings with the carton on your left arm to get a good feel for keeping the arm straight. Then remove the carton and retain that feeling hitting balls. Swinging with only the left arm also is helpful.

A note of caution: a straight left arm does not mean a tense or rigid left arm. The arm should be just firm enough so that it doesn't bend.

Before you throw away your next empty drink carton, ask yourself if putting it on your left arm could improve your golf swing.

USE 3 KEYS TO SOLIDIFY SETUP

You have complete control over your address position on every shot you play, yet almost all of us set up poorly. Your address position is one thing you can work on at home, in front of a mirror. It will be time well spent.

The modern touring professionals have developed a setup position that leads to consistent striking, based on three main points:

1. The knees are cocked toward the target to encourage lively leg action.

2. The right eye is over the right knee to keep the head behind the ball.

3. Most of the weight is on the right foot to eliminate the need for a big weight shift on the backswing.

A great example of this modern address position is Gary Player. Watch how he sets up to the ball the next chance you have. He cocks his knees toward the target, aligns his right eye over his right knee, and sets most of his weight on his right foot, then he hits the bejabbers out of the ball.

Gary Player

HOLD HEAD HIGH FOR FULLER TURN

A couple of years ago a discouraged Kathy Whitworth went to her golf teacher, the venerable Texan Harvey Penick, for help. She had lost distance, lost her ability to maneuver the ball—and lost her confidence.

Penick quickly pinpointed the problem. Whitworth's head was slumped at address, almost down to her chest. She couldn't turn her shoulders and swing freely. She was trapped in a reverse weight shift, her weight going left on the backswing and right on the downswing.

The solution was elementary: keep the head up. Once Whitworth lifted her chin at address, she could turn her shoulders and make an unrestricted swing.

It's old and bad advice to "keep your head down" playing golf; tuck your chin into your chest and you have no chance to swing well. It's better advice, as Kathy Whitworth learned the hard way, to keep your head up.

FLOW INTO YOUR SWING

The golf swing is like a car in that it has to have a starter to get going. You must start your golf swing from motion to make a smooth pass at the ball. All good players make some little preliminary movement to launch the swing. Maybe it's a slight forward press with the hands, like Nancy Lopez... or a slow turning of the head in the direction the shoulders are going to turn, like Jack Nicklaus ... or a small kick with the right knee toward the left, like Gary Player.

Whatever the movement, it serves to warm up your engine. You start your swing relaxed, with a better sense of rhythm. You don't jerk the club away from the ball—a common failing—and immediately kill your tempo.

Flow into the swing rather than start it abruptly. Never be entirely still over the ball. You can't make a smooth golf swing from a standing start. To make a rhythmic swing, develop your own starter movement and repeat it on every shot, always starting your swing from motion.

ADDRESS BALL
WITHOUT
SOLING CLUB

More and more good golfers are addressing the ball with the clubhead off the ground, just above the grass. With a little practice, not soling the club can improve your game. The advantages are several.

First, you tend to grip the club with proper hand pressure. The minimum pressure you need to hold the club off the ground is plenty. Most players grip the club too tightly and lose freedom of motion in their swings.

Another plus to addressing the ball with the clubhead off the ground is a guaranteed clean takeaway. How many times have all of us ruined shots by stubbing the clubhead in the grass on the takeaway? You want to stop your swing and start all over, but some devil possessing you won't hear of it.

Finally, by addressing the ball with the clubhead off the ground, your contact should be crisper. After all, we hit the ball, not the ground behind it, so why not address the ball rather than the ground?

Ben Crenshaw

Jack Nicklaus

SWIVEL HEAD TO FREE UP SWING

One of the hoariest of golf clichés tells us to keep the head still as we swing. Trying to do so is actually a sure way to create tension and weak shots. Lock your head into a fixed position and it's next to impossible to make a free-flowing pass through the ball.

In a good swing the head does move. It doesn't sway dramatically from side to side, but it is allowed to swivel, like an oscillating electric fan on its base. The chin rotates to the right on the backswing, and back to the left on the downswing, for right-handers.

Jack Nicklaus, you may have noticed, always starts his swing with just such a swiveling action of the head. It's controlled and deliberate. To understand what he's doing, envision your head in a box. Your head shouldn't move out of the box, but it should be free to turn within it, as the rest of your upper body turns.

"Keep your head still" is not very good advice. A natural swiveling movement of the head breaks the tension and leads you into a well-coiled backswing.

COCK RIGHT KNEE TO CONTROL WEIGHT SHIFT

Many golfers shift their weight too far to the right on the backswing, then don't get enough weight back to the left on the downswing. They lose power, control—and balance.

In a good weight transfer, the weight goes no farther right on the backswing than the inside of the right foot. Then, coming down, you push off the right foot and move your weight through the ball.

One way to prevent swaying off the ball is to cock your right knee in toward your left at address. At the same time, feel that your right hip and shoulder are "soft" and ready to turn out of the way.

A good practice gimmick is to prop a door wedge under the outside of your right foot and hit shag balls. You can buy a door wedge at your friendly neighborhood hardware store.

One leading teaching professional likes his pupils to literally "get on the ball" to stop swaying. He props a ball under the outside of the student's right foot.

TAKE CLUB STRAIGHT BACK AND THROUGH

Jack Nicklaus believes the key to driving is two feet long. He strives to take the clubhead straight back from the ball for a foot, and keep it moving straight down the line through the ball for a foot.

The first foot of the takeaway largely determines how good a swing you can make. Bring the club straight back from the ball and you're off to a solid start. After that the club comes inside and up.

Through impact, you will improve accuracy if you send the clubhead straight down the line for a foot. This doesn't mean, Nicklaus stresses, that you block the natural release of the club, which should swing back inside the target line after the ball is on its way.

Drive it straight, like Jack Nicklaus, by taking the club straight back from the ball for a foot and swinging it straight down the line for a foot.

SWING BACK PURPOSEFULLY

Consider that the purpose of the backswing in golf is simply to put the club in position for the downswing. There is no hurry, and control is the objective. The idea is to set the club on a good plane and let the club do the work.

Jack Nicklaus takes the club back from the ball so slowly and smoothly you can read the trademark. His backswing is deliberate and designed to store power for his downswing, when he needs it.

Remember that the ball's in no hurry; it can go nowhere until you hit it.

To make a slower backswing, create in advance a mental picture of how you want to look at the top of your swing. Once you know where you're heading, the pressure to rush is removed. All you have to do is take the club back smoothly and put it in position for the downswing. That's the sole purpose of the backswing.

Jack Nicklaus

David Graham

LIFT LEFT HEEL TO EXPAND SWING ARC

David Graham is scarcely larger than his driver—but he's long enough off the tee to stay up with the tour's big hitters. How does he do it?

The Australian-born champ worked long hours to expand his swing arc and generate more distance. He used to make a short upper-body turn, which restricted his swing.

Graham enlarged his swing mainly by letting his left heel come off the ground. Before, he kept it flat, and only an extremely strong and supple player can hold the left heel down and wind up his body enough to hit the ball very far. As we get older, it's more and more difficult to make a big enough swing with the left heel planted.

Graham cautions, "If you do let your left heel come off the ground on your backswing, you must return it to the same place at the start of your downswing. Otherwise you will spin out."

To make a fuller turn and gain distance, let your left heel come up on the backswing as David Graham does.

SWING ON 45-DEGREE PLANE

Hale Irwin's career took off when he made a fundamental improvement in his swing plane. His backswing plane formerly was inconsistent with his downswing plane, which meant he had to make extra moves to compensate. Now his backswing and downswing stay in one plane, a sign of a sound player. If you can swing the club up and down rather much on the same plane, you have gone a long way toward simplifying the golf swing.

How do you find your correct swing plane?

Generally speaking, your best plane is 45 degrees—halfway between vertical and horizontal—running from the ball through the top of your spine. A good way to find it is to address the ball with your feet together and swing to the top with your wrists firm. That should give you a 45-degree plane.

A perfectly upright plane would have the advantage of keeping the club on the target line, while a perfectly horizontal plane would deliver the club exactly at ball level every time. Neither is physically possible, of course, and the 45-degree plane is a happy compromise. That's just about the plane that Hale Irwin's club travels in now that he has improved it.

KEEP IT SLOW—
ESPECIALLY
AT THE TOP

If you had to pick one player in golf whose tempo is worth studying, I would suggest Gene Littler. Littler swings a golf club with the same elegant style that Sinatra brings to a song or Nureyev to a dance. His tempo should be a model for the weekend player.

Here are Gene's main tips on tempo:

Swing all your clubs with the same tempo or pace. Swing your 2-iron as slowly as your 9-iron.

Concentrate on smoothness and rhythm as you prepare for a shot. Take a couple of practice swings and then hit the ball with that same relaxed tempo.

The top of the swing is the most crucial area for good tempo. If you can be going slowly just before you get to the top and just as you start down, your tempo won't be bad.

One more thing. Gene Littler stresses that tempo, like everything else in golf, requires practice.

SWING SHOULDERS UNDER CHIN TO INCREASE POWER

How many golfers can generate two yards off the tee for every pound they weigh? Jack Nicklaus can't, Fuzzy Zoeller can't. But JoAnn Washam on the LPGA Tour can. A mere wisp of a golfer at 120 pounds, she routinely drives the ball 240 yards.

JoAnn's main thought for distance is "Swing the left shoulder under the chin at the top of the swing, and swing the right shoulder under the chin at the bottom."

Swinging the left shoulder under the chin going back gives her a good body coil, she feels, maximizing her shoulder turn while minimizing her hip turn. From there she swings the right shoulder under the chin to ensure a swing path that comes from inside the target line to along the line at impact.

JoAnn Washam

STRETCH TO BUILD A BIGGER TURN

Most weekend golfers don't make a full enough shoulder turn, and the problem is compounded during a layoff if they don't exercise.

Sam Snead credits a big shoulder turn for his nine lives on the golf tour. But Sam enjoys the luxury of playing nearly every day of the year, and the rest of us don't.

But here's an easy Sam Snead exercise that can help your turn. Lay a golf club on your shoulders across the back of your neck, drape your arms up over the club, then have a seat. Now turn your upper body first in one direction, then the other.

Stretch as fully as you can—but if it starts to hurt, don't go farther. Do the exercise 10 times slowly at the first sitting, working up to 50. You will feel your turn get bigger.

The procedure is simple and safe, and Sam swears by it.

SWING WITH LEFT ARM ONLY TO IMPROVE TEMPO

Good tempo in a golf swing may be hard to define, but it's easy to spot, and it sticks out all over tour star Jerry Pate.

Your tempo in golf leaves you when you swing too fast. You jerk the club away from the ball too quickly, then start down from the top too abruptly. By the time you get to the ball it's all you can do to stay in your shoes. How can you find your best tempo? Here is Jerry Pate's answer.

When Pate's tempo is off, he goes to the practice range and works with his short irons alone. He thinks "slow" and simply tries to make solid contact. He strives to eliminate unnecessary movement in his swing, particularly with his hands.

Also to help his tempo, Pate will hit practice balls with his left arm alone. He says the drill, once you master it, makes you use your legs in harmony with your arms, which smoothes out your tempo.

Slow down your tempo Jerry Pate style by practicing with a short iron, some of the time swinging it with the left arm only.

FIRM UP
LEFT-HAND ACTION

You hear a lot of talk about weekend golfers getting too much right hand into their shots. That's a lot of liverwurst according to the top teaching pros I've chatted with on the subject.

It isn't that a right-hander gets too much right hand into the shot, it's that he doesn't get enough left hand into it. The idea is to firm up your left-hand action, then hit hard with the right and at the bottom of the swing.

Pull the club through the ball with your left hand, instead of throwing it with the right hand. Keep the back of the left hand facing the target. It's as if the left hand and right hand are running a race, and the left hand wins. You'll hit the ball farther—and just as straight.

Most of us are naturally stronger with our right hands. To build up the left hand, practice swinging a club with the left hand only, or squeeze a rubber ball when you're watching golf on television. On the course, grip more firmly with the last three fingers of the left hand.

Remember, if your left hand is in control, you can't get too much right hand into the shot.

Laura Baugh

ROLL FOREARMS TO HIT OFFENSIVE BLOW

Most golfers could play dramatically better if they struck the ball with an offensive blow. You do that when the toe of the club passes the heel through the impact area. The most common bad shot in golf is the slice, and the slicer's club is open at impact, or looking to the right. The quickest way to stop slicing is to close the face of the club through the ball.

You can understand the principle if you've played table tennis. The forehand slam in table tennis is an offensive blow and it's the strongest shot you can hit.

You strike an offensive blow in golf by rolling the face of the club closed, with your forearms—not your shoulders or hands, which are too active in a slice swing. Hitting an offensive blow with your forearms, you produce the greatest amount of power with the least amount of effort. In addition to the obvious benefit of added distance, the offensive swing contributes to a more positive attitude overall. You will like being able to attack the course.

To hit an offensive blow in golf, make the toe of the club pass the heel through impact by rotating the forearms.

KEEP BACK OF LEFT HAND SQUARE TO TARGET

If the weekend golfer can learn one thing from Lee Trevino, it's how to move through the ball.

Lee has an unorthodox golf swing—but a classic action through the ball. Even Ben Hogan says so, and he passes out compliments rarely. Trevino likes to imagine he's back-handing a wall with his left hand as he swings through the contact zone. "If the back of my hand is square to the target," he reasons, "the clubhead will be, too."

Trevino tries to swing the clubhead down the target line well past the ball. He can give the impression, as Hogan could, of keeping the clubface on the ball for several feet. It doesn't really happen, but every little bit of extension helps accuracy.

Through the ball, Trevino's legs drive toward the target but his head stays back, so that his body looks like an inverted letter "C".

Andy Bean

POUR ON CLUBHEAD SPEED IN 'ZIP ZONE'

A good golfer is much more swing conscious than ball conscious. He's aware of the ball, and keeps his eye on it, but he knows that, if he makes a sound swing the ball will simply get in the way of the club.

Swing through the ball and the results take care of themselves. Become "ball-bound" and you're inhibited right away from turning and coiling well. You won't generate enough clubhead speed.

At the bottom of the swing, in the "zip zone" as it's been called, the clubhead should be picking up velocity. If it is, the momentum will carry you through to a good full finish. When a good player completes his swing, his belt buckle is facing the target.

A trusty way to encourage swinging through the ball is to think about the finish of your swing as you prepare to hit a shot. Fix a picture in your mind of a model follow-through. By concentrating on finishing your swing at the outset, you will whip the club through the ball—and finish what you start with your swing.

HIT THROUGH, NOT TO, THE BALL

A good golfer merely lets the ball get in the way of his swing. That's how a small man like Larry Nelson, all 150 pounds of him, can drive a ball 270 yards. He sweeps his arms freely out toward the target into an unrestricted follow-through. The typical weekend player hits to the ball instead of through it and loses clubhead speed just when he needs it most—in the impact area.

Bear in mind that a golf ball weighs only 1.62 ounces. If you weigh just 150 pounds, that's 1,480 times the weight of the ball you're striking.

You don't need to pack all your strength into your swing. Forget about hitting hard and swing rhythmically through the ball. It will go farther. To get the feeling of swinging through the ball, practice hitting shots with your eyes closed. Swing your arms down freely with no jerking, or tenseness, or extra effort. On your good shots, notice how light the ball feels coming off the clubface. That's only because it is.

Larry Nelson

John Mahaffey

'HIT THE SKY' ON YOUR FINISH

At 5 feet 9 and 150 pounds, John Mahaffey is scarcely larger than his 3-wood. How does he hit the ball far enough to compete on tour and what can we learn from him?

One reason John Mahaffey can move a golf ball so far is that he finishes what he starts with his swing. Most weekend golfers lose 20 yards off the tee because they swing to the ball instead of through it; they fail to follow through.

Mahaffey stresses that following through is as vital swinging a driver as it is hitting a baseball, throwing a football or shooting a basketball. "Weekend players don't follow through better because they attempt to 'steer' the clubhead," he says. "They don't 'release' the clubhead through the hitting zone and let it zip through the ball."

Mahaffey finds it helpful to envision a complete follow-through before he starts to swing. As he addresses the ball he will see in his mind's eye a full finish, with the hands nice and high. He thinks of trying to 'hit the sky' with his hands.

To hit through the ball instead of to it, and get more distance on your drives, visualize a full follow-through before you swing.

2.
SHOT
MAKING TIPS

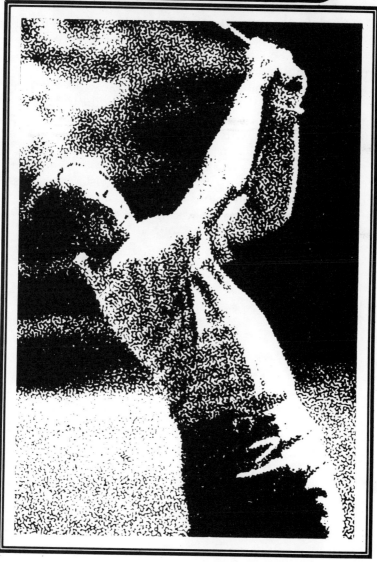

SWING FAIRWAY WOOD LIKE 9-IRON

The tendency on a long fairway wood shot in golf is to swing harder trying for extra distance—and get revolting results. You hit behind the ball, or top it, and the shot winds up dismayingly short of the green.

The next time you take a fairway wood, try this different approach. Instead of thinking about hitting the ball 220 yards, think about hitting it only half that distance. Swing your fairway wood with the same tempo you'd use on a 9-iron shot, when distance isn't a factor.

Just because you have a long wood shot to the green, you don't have to swing with hurricane force. Distance results from swinging smoothly and making clean contact.

Try to hit your fairway woods only half as far as you need to and you'll reach your target more often.

Hale Irwin

Tom Weiskopf

SWING LONG IRONS NO HARDER

Long irons are the curse of the weekend golfer's game, but they don't have to be.

Long irons require no more effort than short irons. If you do swing them the same way you swing the short irons—no harder, no faster—you'll be pleasantly surprised by the results. Tom Weiskopf is probably the world's best long-iron player. He stresses that he does absolutely nothing differently with his long irons.

Don't be intimidated by a long iron's design. The face is relatively straight and shaft is longer, but that doesn't mean you have to help the club get the ball up in the air. Manufacturers build plenty of loft into a long iron: a standard 3-iron carries 24 degrees of loft. Swing it smoothly down through the ball and trust the club to do its thing.

A good practice tactic is to take turns hitting balls with a short iron and a long iron, keeping your tempo consistent. Hit a half dozen shots with a 9-iron. Alternate the two clubs to ingrain the feeling of a consistent swing pace, and if you start to press on your long-iron shots, switch immediately to the short iron.

If you want results approaching the likes of Tom Weiskopf, do as he does and swing your long irons the same way you swing your short irons.

VARY YOUR FOCAL POINT DEPENDING ON THE SHOT

U.S. Open champion Hale Irwin is a deadly iron player. To hit crisp iron shots, he finds it helpful to change his focal point on the ball for different types of approach shots, and commends the idea to the rest of us.

On a full iron shot, Irwin focuses on the top of the ball. On pitch shots and chip shots he looks at the front of the ball.

You might think you'd top the ball this way, but consider that most iron shots are struck "fat"—we watch the back of the ball and hit behind it. Irwin wants us to hit the ball before we hit the ground. He points out that if you don't meet the ball squarely, you usually are better off catching it "thin" than "fat"; you at least have a better chance to get the ball up to the hole.

So to hit iron shots more crisply, focus on the top of the ball for full approach shots and on the front of the ball for pitch and chip shots.

MOVE BALL UP, HANDS BACK TO HIT HIGH IRON SHOTS

Almost all golfers go through spells when they feel low because they cannot hit the ball high with their irons. If you can hit high iron shots in golf you can aim the ball at the flag without worrying that it will bounce over the green. Players like Jack Nicklaus and Tom Watson win major championships largely because they can hit high, soft-landing iron shots. They carry the trouble that fronts modern greens and set themselves up for birdie putts.

You can make two small but crucial adjustments in your address position to get higher shots: move the ball slightly forward in your stance and move your hands slightly back.

Then the key during the swing is to "stay down to the ball"—don't let your upper body come up before the ball is gone. Actor Jim Garner, a zealous golfer, summons a helpful mental image when he wants to hit an iron shot high. He imagines that the ball must clear a tall tree directly in his path. That helps him stay down with the shot.

If you have trouble trajecting your iron shots high enough, move the ball slightly forward and your hands slightly back. Ball forward, hands back. Then imagine, like Jim Garner, that you need to hit the ball over a tall tree.

SWING WITH EASE AGAINST A BREEZE

The natural tendency playing in the wind is to swing harder. It also is the worst.

There are at least three good reasons not to swing hard in the wind.

1. When you swing hard you tend to make poor contact.
2. Wind threatens your balance, and a hard swing makes it more difficult to keep your balance.
3. Even if you make good contact and stay in balance swinging hard, you apply added spin to the ball, and it climbs too high, especially into the wind.

In a crosswind, the first principle is to use it and not let it use you. Aim to the windward side of your target and let the wind move the ball in toward the target.

Keep in mind too that higher numbered woods can be wild in the wind—you're better off keeping the ball down with your long irons, something most of us do all too well.

Swing with ease against a breeze. It may not be great poetry, but it's great advice.

Tom Watson

BUILD STANCE THAT CONFORMS TO SLOPE

Don't let sloping lies throw you off balance. On a hilly lie your swing doesn't change but your stance does. Basically you build a stance that conforms to the slope, so you can make a normal swing.

If the ball is below your feet on the side of a hill, stand closer to the ball. Keep your knees flexed and your weight back toward your heels so you won't fall forward. If the ball is above your feet, reverse the procedure. Grip down on the club and set your weight toward your toes.

For uphill and downhill lies, play the ball off your high foot, keep your weight balanced and swing along the slope of the hill.

On any hilly lie, a practice swing is vital, to find where the club will meet the ground.

Having said all that, avoidance is the better part of valor on shots from hilly lies. Aim at flat areas of the fairway. But if you do get an uneven lie, remember to build a stance that conforms to the slope.

PUNCH BALL
OUT OF DIVOT HOLES

They say old Harry Vardon, who more or less invented the modern golf grip, was so accurate that when he played twice in a day his shots in the afternoon would finish in his divot marks from the morning. You and I don't have that problem, but it is hard to get through a round without facing the challenge of a shot from somebody's divot mark. You handle it differently than a shot from a good lie.

First, take one more club than normal if your ball is in a divot, because the ball won't fly as far. If you normally would use a 6-iron, take a 5.

Choke down on the grip and set up so the ball is back toward your right foot if you're righthanded, with your weight favoring your left side. Set your hands ahead of the clubface at address and be sure they lead the face through the hitting area. Then simply "punch" the ball, with an abbreviated swing.

It helps to imagine you are hitting under the branches of a tree, even if the nearest tree is in the next county.

If your ball is in a divot mark, take one more club, position your weight and hands left, and hit a punch shot. Harry Vardon would be proud.

TAKE IT EASY
OUT OF ROUGH

Lou Graham finds that the weekend golfers he plays with in pro-ams share a common failing: they try to hit the ball too hard out of the rough. He admonishes us to take it easy in the rough.

The harder you swing in the rough, the worse off you are—because you overuse your right side and make poor contact. "Making good contact is the most important thing in the rough," says Graham, "and the way to make good contact is with a smooth, controlled swing."

To encourage good contact and keep too much grass from getting between the clubface and the ball, stand a little closer to the ball and move it back a couple of inches in your stance.

Select a club with enough loft to escape the rough for sure. Don't try to reach the green if you're a long way out, just concentrate on getting the ball out of the rough in one shot.

Take it from Lou Graham, the smart way to play shots in the rough is to take it easy.

Lou Graham

USE LOFTED WOOD FROM NORMAL ROUGH

Jack Nicklaus is a great player out of the rough in part because he is tremendously strong. His advice to the average golfer is to rely more on cool thinking than strength that he probably lacks.

Jack suggests you will do better on long shots from normal rough with a 4- or 5-wood than a long iron. The rounded sole of the lofted wood slides through the tall grass more readily than the straight, sharp leading edge of the long iron.

If your lie is poor, Jack recommends opening the face of the club and making an upright swing so you can hit abruptly down into the ball without a lot of interference from the grass.

If your lie is poorer than poor, you may simply have to chop the ball back into the fairway with a wedge. The cardinal principle of playing from the rough is to get out with your first stroke, no matter how much distance you have to sacrifice.

But on long shots from a reasonable lie in the rough, take Jack's advice and use a lofted wood rather than a long iron.

TRY 'TROUBLE WOOD' FOR RECOVERY SHOTS

The "trouble wood," as it's called in the trade, is the most innovative club to come along since the sand wedge, and many pro golfers are carrying it. A trouble wood can be an even more valuable weapon for the average player.

Built for all manner of bad lies, trouble woods are easier to play than fairway woods or long irons because the weight is distributed lower in the clubhead and the face is more lofted. You can launch the ball quickly and high, even from heavy rough, downhill lies or fairway bunkers. And you can handle these difficult recovery shots without changing your swing; the club makes the adjustment for you if you play the ball back slightly in your stance to strike a more descending blow.

Potential drawbacks to trouble woods are diminished effectiveness in the wind and inconsistent distance. But for most golfers, the pluses of delivering the ball higher and straighter from bad lies far outweigh the minuses.

ADJUST THE TEE HEIGHT TO SHAPE YOUR SHOTS

A seemingly minor factor like how you tee a golf ball can affect your swing plane and the shape of your shots.

The higher you tee the ball, the flatter you will tend to swing; the lower you tee the ball, the more upright you will tend to swing. Consequently, the higher you tee it, the easier it is to hook the ball, and the lower you tee it the easier it is to fade. If you slice, you may be teeing too low.

A good rule of thumb for driver shots is to tee the ball so half of it shows above the top of the driver.

Contrary to popular belief, teeing the ball higher will not necessarily make you hit it higher. To make your drives go higher, tee the ball lower and hit it with more of a descending blow.

We owe a debt to Dr. William Lowell, a New Jersey dental surgeon, for inventing the wood tee in 1920. It brings to mind a line from Ring Lardner: "I am undecided," he said, "what is the toughest shot in golf. It is either an unconceded 3-foot putt, or the explosion shot off the first tee."

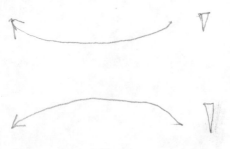

3.
SHORT
GAME TIPS

CHIP COINS TO BUILD MONEY-WINNING SHORT GAME

Severiano Ballesteros, the swashbuckling Spaniard who won the Masters at age 23, learned to play by chipping pesetas (coins) in the caddieyard with a hand-me-down iron. As a result, though today Seve is known as a long driver, the more telling side of his game is getting the ball close to the hole from around the green. He is a great chipper.

With practice, anyone can become at least a good chipper. Steal a trick from Seve's formative years and practice by chipping coins at a target with a short iron. If you can make clean contact with a coin, meeting a golf ball squarely is routine stuff.

Keep the chipping stroke short and crisp. Set your weight and hands ahead of the ball, then hold the left wrist firm through impact. If there is one single key to chipping, it is that firm left wrist through the ball—don't let it collapse.

Chipping coins the way Ballesteros did as a youngster will help you win more $1 nassaus this season!

SHOOT 'BASKETS' WITH YOUR FAVORITE CHIPPING IRON

Foul weather can stop you from working on your driving, but not from sharpening your chipping. You'll save more strokes with the latter, anyway. Five minutes a day of chipping practice could knock five shots off the average weekender's game.

You can set up an indoor chipping area in almost any room in the house. You need only a slice of artificial turf—a $5 doormat simulates grass—and a target, like a basket. Concentrate on making a short, smooth backswing, keeping the left wrist firm. Then accelerate your arms down into and through the ball. Vary the length of your shots. Make up a contest: see how many "baskets" you can make in 15 tries.

CHIP WITH LESS-LOFTED CLUBS

Until she came on tour, Nancy Lopez did most of her chipping with a wedge. She soon noticed that the pros were chipping with less lofted-clubs, and getting the ball closer to the hole. Lopez would rather switch than lose, and she began chipping with an 8-iron instead of her wedge. Her scoring improved dramatically.

Chipping with a less lofted-club, she could land the ball on the green sooner and let it run to the hole. She learned to turn her chips into putts as soon as possible, and now gets the ball "up and down" in two strokes from the fringe with awesome regularity.

The average golfer misses many more greens than a Nancy Lopez, and can profit from her experience. Take a less lofted club for your chips—there is nothing wrong with dropping down to a middle iron—and run the ball to the hole.

Nancy Lopez

Lon Hinkle

USE SAND WEDGE TO INCREASE PITCHING CONTROL

225 ft.

Touring professionals and top amateur golfers often pitch with a sand wedge from 75 yards on in. There is a good deal to be said for the practice. An approach shot with a sand wedge climbs higher and lands softer than the same shot with a pitching wedge. From a good grass lie, you have more control.

The added weight of the club helps produce the shot with less effort. The construction of the head gives better results if you hit behind the ball—a frequent failing of weekend players.

Using the sand wedge off grass takes practice, like any other new shot, but don't think of it as special. Swing no differently than you would with a pitching wedge. The only adjustments you might make are in your setup. Move the ball back slightly in your stance and set your weight and hands slightly forward, to be sure you hit the ball before you hit the turf.

Your first few pitch shots with a sand wedge may well come up short. With the sand wedge you can aim right down the top of the flagstick—an advantage once you're used to it. Experiment on the practice range to find your maximum pitching distance with the sand wedge—it may be closer to 50 yards than to the 75 the pros get.

TRY PUTTER FROM FRINGE

Most weekend players chip from the fringe, but a putt is the better percentage shot. The touring pros can finesse the ball with a variety of cute little wedge shots—you and I can't, consistently.

If you're more than 10 feet off the green and the fringe grass is short and smooth, take your putter. The ball behaves more predictably on the ground. Also you're more accustomed to putting than to chipping.

Make the same stroke you would make if the ball were on the green, putting the ball just slightly harder than normal. The fringe probably will not affect the shot as much as you think. If it's well-manicured, the ball will run along the top of the grass onto the green.

Try this quick test before your next round. Putt a dozen shots from the fringe around the practice green, then chip a dozen. See if you aren't more consistent putting than chipping from the fringe.

Bob Murphy

CALIBRATE BACKSWING TO VARY PITCH SHOT

Weekend golfers frequently waste strokes on pitch shots because they don't know how big a swing to take with the wedge.

Most golfers use the same long swing for pitch shots from 25 yards that they use from 75 yards, let up at impact—and muff the shot. Or else they use a 25-yard swing for a 75-yard shot—and fall far shot.

How far back should you bring the club on shots from 25 yards, 50 yards, 75 yards? Here are three rules of thumb (or hand) that you can modify on the practice range to suit your game. The objective in all cases is to accelerate the club into the ball.

—From 25 yards, your hands should get no higher than your hip.

—From 50 yards, the hands will be about shoulder high.

—From 75 yards with a wedge you're making nearly a full swing and the hands will be head high.

Backswing length on pitch shots must vary—so you can make a firm, accelerating swing.

IMAGINE HIGH GRASS TO ESCAPE FROM SAND

Most weekend golfers have heard all the traditional advice for getting out of sand a hundred times—and they still have trouble with the strangeness of bunker shots.

One 16-handicapper I know could have been stranded in the Mojave Desert for all the luck he had in bunkers. Then a pro told him to pretend in the sand that he had a little pitch shot from high grass around the green, where he would take a relaxed swing and scoop under the ball. By playing sand shots as though they were pitch shots from high grass, that 16-handicapper's bunker play improved to the point he's now a 13.

It isn't always necessary, either, to use the sand wedge in the sand. Pick the simplest club you can, starting with the straight-faced putter if there's no lip on the trap and the sand is firm.

One more point about sand play. Since you can't ground the club in the hazard, take a couple of nice full practice swings before you get in the bunker, preferably in high grass. Then play the sand shot as if you were still in that grass.

KEEP HEEL OF CLUB AHEAD OF TOE ON BUNKER SHOTS

How do you play a sand shot in golf? Well, one expert player suggests you open the blade and swing to the left of your target.

And a well-known teacher stresses the importance of never allowing the left wrist to break down.

An equally esteemed teacher emphasizes working the right hand under the ball.

Who's right? While it sounds impossible, they all are. Apparently contradictory methods for getting out of sand have one key principle in common: the toe of the club does not pass the heel through the impact area.

To learn the technique of keeping the heel of the club ahead of the toe, practice in grass just off the green, or in your backyard. Hit short pitch shots with your sand wedge and concentrate on keeping the face from closing. Think of the face of your sand wedge pointing to the sky until it's hip high in your follow-through.

Regardless of your method, you can play decently from sand by adhering to one dictum: the toe of the club must not pass the heel through impact.

Tom Kite

4.
PUTTING TIPS

APPROACH EACH PUTT WITH SAME REGIMEN

The top putters in golf over the years invariably have followed a pre-stroke routine. Bobby Locke, who won the British Open four times and may have been the best of them all, is a classic example. A great putter like Locke might consistently take two practice strokes and use 10 seconds to putt. The key is that he follows the same regimen every time he lines up a putt, takes his stance and leads into the stroke. It is a countdown approach that can help the weekend player.

The main advantage of pattern putting is being able to get the putter in motion better. There is no lag between preliminaries and stroke, no time for the muscles to tense and the mind to churn out negative thoughts. Your routine takes over for you under pressure and eases you into the stroke.

If following a programmed method seems depressingly mechanical, it is worth it in consistency. Nothing is more depressing than stabbing a five-foot putt five feet past the hole with five dollars at stake.

Pattern putting characterizes the great putters and can give you more steadiness on the greens.

Bobby Locke

MAKE 'EM QUICK

Most golfers would putt better if they putted quicker. The longer you stand over a putt in golf, the more chance your nerves have to upset your stroke. You need to keep your body still while putting, and that can lead to tension after more than a few seconds.

Also, if you dawdle over a putt you can start second-guessing yourself; your first impressions of a putt usually are your best. Determine before you set up to the ball the line of the putt and how hard to hit it.

Then address the ball with your mind made up. Your one thought should be simply to start the ball rolling well. The first six inches of a putt are the most important, so stroke the ball solidly and don't worry about the results.

Notice how decisively and quickly good putters like Ben Crenshaw and Lee Trevino address and stroke the ball. They believe that the longer you stand over a putt, the worse your chances are. You probably will putt better if you putt quicker.

THE PRAYING GRIP

From a distance, good putters may appear to hold the club differently. But up close their grips share a crucial feature all of us should emulate.

Most top putters hold the club with the palms of the hands facing each other. The right palm and the back of the left hand look down the line of the putt. This way the hands work together, as a unit. The putterhead stays square to the arc of the stroke, with no wristy manipulation necessary.

A good way to assume a palms-facing grip is to put the hands together in a 'praying' position, then slide them onto the putter handle. That works for good putters—and it can work for you.

CHOKE DOWN TO UPGRADE STROKE

Most of us putt poorly because we overuse our hands and wrists. There is no quicker way to undermine your scoring.

A good drill to firm up your putting stroke is to putt with a shortened grip. Shift your grip down on the putter until the handle end of the club is lodged against your left forearm, if you're right-handed. Now practice-putt keeping the handle in touch with the forearm. If it pulls away, you're breaking down.

A few minutes of practicing with a shortened grip will convince you that a stroke made mainly with the arms and shoulders and less with the hands and wrists is more solid and repeatable.

To firm up your putting, use the short-grip drill, choking down on the putter until the handle is pressing against your left forearm, and holding the putter there during the stroke.

KEEP HEAD STONE-STILL ON PUTTS

If your putting goes awry, check your head first. It must remain steady. One touring professional I know keeps his head still by getting over the ball and imagining he is a block of granite.

The only parts of your body you want to move are your arms and hands. Keep as quiet as possible otherwise, especially with your head.

The head is the heaviest part of the body. If it moves, so does something else. We all have a tendency to "wish" a putt toward the hole by moving the head with the stroke; or we like to give a putt a little "body English"; or we want to look up and see where the ball's going.

That's OK once you've struck the putt, but the costly movement usually starts sooner than that. Sam Snead, the ageless one, has always tried to keep his head down putting until he hears the ball rattle into the bottom of the cup. There is no sweeter sound in the world, and you'll hear it more often if you putt with a steady head.

PUTT LIKE
STATUE OF LIBERTY

"Gentle Ben" Crenshaw has been known to sway off the ball on his full swing—but there is no sway in his putting stroke, the best on the pro tour. He has developed a remarkable ability to keep his head and body still as he's putting, even from 40 and 50 feet. That's why he's so consistent on the greens.

His stroke is made mostly with the arms and only a slight wrist break. An arm stroke promotes stability, and Crenshaw is as stable over the ball as the Statue of Liberty.

He allows his arms to swing the putterhead away from the ball, along and then inside the target line, and return it to square at impact.

This is the classical "swinging gate" method that most good putters use. Its single most impressive feature, exemplified by Ben Crenshaw, is a steady head and body, and all of us can learn from that.

FEEL PUTTS WITH YOUR THUMBS

The best putter in golf is not Jack Nicklaus or Ben Crenshaw or Nancy Lopez. He is the venerable George Low.

Low played the tour years ago—until he found he could make more money on the practice green than Ben Hogan could make winning tournaments. Today George teaches the stars how to putt.

He has three simple keys.

1. Feel with your thumbs. If you don't believe you feel through your thumbs, George suggests reaching in your pocket and picking out a coin. You're feeling the coin essentially with your thumb, right?

Put both thumbs on top of a flat-topped grip—and pull them up short for maximum feel.

2. Anchor your weight on the left heel.

3. Stroke like a swinging gate. A gate opens and closes square to its arc, and so should the putting stroke, according to George Low. That's the low-down on putting from the acknowledged master.

Bob Charles

PUTT LIKE A PENDULUM

Bob Charles' putting stroke could be a model for the weekend golfer because it's simple and repeatable. The New Zealand pro believes the stroke should resemble a pendulum. The arms and club swing at a smooth, even tempo, the clubface square to the path of the stroke throughout.

He feels that the arms and putter should function as a one-piece unit, the putter swinging from the shoulders because it's an extension of the arms. He takes his wrists out of the stroke so it has fewer moving parts.

The pendulum analogy holds in that a true pendulum gradually swings upward—and so does Charles' putter. He makes no effort to keep the club close to the ground going back or coming through.

Charles' only departure from the action of a true pendulum is to accelerate the club into the ball, to insure crisp hits.

PLAY EVERY PUTT STRAIGHT

Every putt in golf can be a straight putt—if you know how to handle it, says Bobby Locke, one of the best putters in history. He doesn't mean straight at the hole; he means straight at an imaginary target you select after calculating the break in the putt.

Most golfers fail to pick a target on breaking putts—they aim at the hole and then try to compensate with an unnatural stroke. The results can be pretty unnatural too. Pick a target to the side of the hole from which the ball will break, and line up to hit the ball at that spot. Aim the blade of your putter at your make-believe target and align your feet and body parallel to your new target line. Finally, be sure your last glance before you launch into your stroke is at your imaginary target, not the hole.

Once you adjust your aim and alignment this way, every putt does become a straight putt.

PUTT TO SPOT
BEHIND HOLE

Nancy Lopez says the big difference between her putting and the average golfer's putting is aggressiveness. She thinks most golfers are far too timid on the greens and makes this suggestion to develop aggressiveness regardless of your gender:

"Be sure you don't leave putts short. Visualize an imaginary hole a foot behind the real one. Then putt to the imaginary hole!"

Nancy stresses that it's much better to leave a putt a foot long than a foot short. By getting it to the hole it has a chance to go in. One pseudo-scientific study shows you have to hit a 12-foot putt that hard on the average green to make it anyway.

To avoid committing the unpardonable golfing sin of leaving putts short, work with Nancy's drill of visualizing an imaginary hole a foot behind the real one, and putting for that imaginary hole.

A SIMPLE 'PUSH PULL' STROKE

If your putting is inconsistent and costing you too many strokes, here's an easy-to-remember instant lesson: use a simplified push-pull stroke.

The left hand should guide the putting stroke. The right hand supplies power and touch but the left hand leads and steers, and that's why an uncomplicated push-pull stroke is reliable.

A firm left hand starts the backstroke and starts the through-stroke back to the ball. Think of pushing the putter away from the ball with the left hand, then pulling it back through with the left hand. "Push-pull." Don't clutter your mind with any other mechanical thoughts on the golf course.

A good practice gambit is to putt with only the left hand on the club. Be sure to accelerate the putterhead through the ball. From three and four feet try to send the putterhead into the hole, hard on the heels of the ball.

To put consistency in your putting, try the push-pull stroke. Push the putter away with the left hand and pull it through with the left hand.

USE RIGHT TOE
TO GAUGE
LENGTH OF STROKE

Tom Watson's putting philosophy boils down to two simple thoughts: acceleration and solid contact.

When Watson steps up to a putt, he thinks only of accelerating the putter through the ball and making solid contact. If he can do those two things, he reasons, he will putt well and win tournaments.

By acceleration, he means the putterhead is gaining speed at impact. Most putting problems are caused by deceleration at impact, which makes the putter waver weakly off line. To counter that tendency, Watson makes sure his follow-through is longer than his backswing. He says a good orientation point is the right big toe. Take the putter back as far as your right toe, accelerate through the ball, and see how far the putt rolls. From there, gauge the length of your backswing for putts of different distances—adjusting how far inside or outside your right toe you should swing the putter. Always follow-through farther than you took it back.

To make good putting contact, Watson invokes Bobby Jones' old mental trick of visualizing a tiny tack sticking out the back of the ball—then he just drives the tack into the ball.

TRY CROSS- HANDED GRIP TO STEADY STROKE

Touring pro Bruce Lietzke believes his cross-handed putting can make considerable sense for the typical weekend player who he says is prone to using wrists and hands too much in the putting stroke.

"Cross-handed putting puts the left hand in command of the stroke," Lietzke contends. Crossing the hands—placing the right hand on top if you're right handed—should firm up your stroke. You should find it easier to stroke from the shoulders, and accelerate the putter toward the target.

Lietzke finds the cross-handed grip extremely helpful on putts inside 10 feet. He also recommends it as a useful practice tactic to develop a dominant left hand.

Bruce Lietzke

ENLARGE TARGET ON LONG PUTTS

Most three-putt greens are brought on by trying too hard to sink the original long putt. "Lower your expectations and lighten the pressure," says former Masters champion Tommy Aaron, a Georgia boy made good and one of the best lag putters in the game.

Aaron visualizes a wagon wheel around the cup and settles for simply rolling the ball anywhere inside the wheel. "You will be amazed," he says, "how many more long putts you make when you don't try so hard."

Aaron works with two stroking keys when outside 20 feet. He pauses at the end of his backswing to get every-thing together for the through-swing, and he strives to finish his stroke low with the putterhead on the grass. But first he dismisses the idea of sinking a long putt and merely tries to roll the ball into a wagon wheel.

If that imagery doesn't work for you, try visualizing a sunken hot tub or the like. Take the fear out of long, hard putts by enlarging your target.

SURVEY
BREAKING PUTTS
EARLY ON

Reading breaking putts can be harder than reading Einstein equations for weekend golfers who don't know what to look for. Begin by surveying your putt before you ever get to the green. As you walk up to a green, quickly note its general slope, because your putt will tend to roll with that slope. Getting this lay of the land will help you see through optical illusions on hilly courses.

On the green, weekend golfers often exaggerate the break in a putt. From eight feet and closer, you seldom face a putt that breaks so much you should aim outside the cup.

Also consider the speed of the green on breaking putts. A putt on a fast green will break more than a putt on a slow green will. The grain of the green—the direction the grass is growing—is a final factor to evaluate.

On breaking putts, then, survey the general slope of the green, guard against reading too much break into short putts, and don't forget to figure the speed and grain of the green.

PUTTING
FAST GREENS

Jack Nicklaus believes fast greens, like those in the major championships, are the best test of putting. Not coincidentally, he is the best fast-greens putter in the world.

Nicklaus stresses that it is vital at a course with fast greens to allow yourself a few unhurried minutes before your round to practice-putt. The pros always do this, but weekend players many times do not.

Nicklaus recommends practice-putting from different distances, with the emphasis on your makeable putts—the ones from 12 feet in.

Then on fast greens out on the course, Nicklaus is careful not to leave himself tricky downhill second putts. He guesses that more major championships have been lost on short downhill second putts than any other way. He plans his first putt so that if he misses, the next one will be uphill.

On fast greens, then, Jack Nicklaus allows himself extra time to practice-putt before a round—and plans his first putt so he leaves himself an uphill second putt if he misses. We should try the same approach.

Jack Nicklaus

STUDY GRAIN
BEFORE YOU PUTT

To be a good putter, you have to be able to read grain—especially if you play golf in the south or west on Bermuda-grass greens. It isn't as difficult as reading "War and Peace," but it isn't easy.

One touring pro says the grain on a green is like the hair on your head; it lays whichever way it's cut and combed. In any event, grain can have a dramatic effect on your putts, and you need to know how to identify it. Putting with the grain, the ball will roll faster; putting against the grain, you must stroke more firmly. Cross-grain putts are tricky, because the grain will move the ball in the direction the grain is lying.

When you assess grain, try to get the sun to your back. If the grass is shiny in the sunlight, you're putting with the grain. But if the grass appears dull or ragged, the grain is into you. Checking the grass on the edges of the cup also can be informative.

Know that, generally speaking, grain runs toward water. Grain also follows the sun, like the touring pros. Bermuda grass will run west, to get that last bit of sunlight each day.

EVALUATE PUTTS FROM THE LOW SIDE

Of the two dimensions in putting—distance and direction—distance is more crucial. And the longer the putt, the more crucial judging distance becomes.

On longer putts, your natural instincts take care of judging the direction; it's like sighting a gun. Distance is the key. If you make the ball go the required distance, you can be four feet off line and the ball is still going to stop only four feet from the hole. Without a good idea of the distance, you might putt the ball on line but come up 10 feet short or long. Good putters have a knack for making the ball travel the proper distance—that's how you keep from three-putting.

An important aid in judging distance is triangulation—looking at the putt from the low side midway between the ball and the cup. If you want to determine the length of a pencil, you don't look at it from one end to the other, you hold it sideways and look at it. The same is true for a putt.

Distance is more important than direction in putting, and the best gauge of distance is to look at the putt from the low side, halfway to the hole.

Lee Trevino

SCOUT PUTT FROM DIFFERENT ANGLES— BUT QUICKLY

Lee Trevino stalks his putts as seriously as a lion tamer circling his beasts. He believes you can't study a putt from too many angles.

Most of us sight down the line of the putt and let it go at that. We address the ball with an uncertain attitude and make an uncertain stroke. Trevino likes to size up a putt from both ends and the middle, the low side to be exact, figuring he'll see something from beyond the hole he didn't notice from behind the ball, and something from the side he didn't see from there. He also observes the grass around the cup to find which way it's growing, because that will influence the ball as it dies.

When you check a putt from different vantage points, do it quickly so you won't hold up play. Bear in mind that no one launches a putt any faster than Lee "cover-all-the-angles" Trevino. Begin your surveying as soon as you reach the green, while your playing partners prepare to putt. Then when it's your turn you'll be ready to go.

ADD WEIGHT TO PUTTER FOR SMOOTHER STROKE

Over 17 oz

If your putting stroke is less than smooth, here's a suggestion: use a heavier putter. You'll have a better chance to make a solid stroke because your tempo will be slower and smoother. On rough greens you also would be able to roll the ball better.

Most putters on the market today weigh between 16 and 17 ounces. When you get over 17, you're in the "heavy" category. Experiment with putters over 17 ounces and see if you don't firm up your stroke.

What if you decide you need a heavier putter, but you like the looks of your old one, battered though it may be? How can you add weight to it?

The easiest way is to apply lead tape to the back of the putterhead. That's what many tour pros do when they play a course with slow greens. Most home professionals have rolls of lead tape in their shops, and hardware stores also carry it.

However you arrive at one, a heavier putter definitely can help even the worst basket cases on the green.

5.
TACTICS ON THE COURSE

PERCENTAGE GOLF DEFINED

We hear a lot about "playing the percentages" in golf from the stars on tour and from teachers. But what does that really mean to you and me?

To play percentage golf, consider what will happen if the shot doesn't turn out quite the way you want it to. Ask yourself where the ball is going to wind up if you don't hit your best shot, particularly on your approach into the green. If you miss your target, what chance will you have to get up and down in two strokes?

For example: if the pin is tucked close to the left side of an elevated green and you miss to the left, you'll face a shot up the bank and have very little green to work with. You probably won't be able to get the ball close. So you shouldn't aim at the flag with your approach. Just try to get the ball in the center of the green and settle for your par—or your bogey, as the case may be.

That's an example of playing percentage golf, which means in essence: consider what will happen if you miss.

PLAY HEADS UP

"Golf is a game of intelligence often played stupidly," says star teaching professional Bob Toski. He believes you can knock strokes off your handicap simply by thinking your way around the course better.

Start by knowing when to attack the course and when to play defensively. Every hole has its weak and strong points. Find out where they are and attack the weak areas. If there's a bunker on the right and you're not a good bunker player, shade yourself to the left. Allow for error. If you don't, you're just hitting and hoping.

Plan a hole from the cup back, not from the tee forward. Learn to hit the ball where it will be easiest to make your next shot.

Consider the side on which to miss the green. It might seem defensive, but it pays to assess the trouble in case you don't split the flag with your approach.

Judy Rankin

BE CAUTIOUS OFF TEE, AGGRESSIVE TO GREEN

One big reason Judy Rankin became the first $100,000-a-year player in the history of the LPGA Tour is her skill at course management—thinking her way around the course. Her basic strategy has always been to play defensively off the tee and aggressively into the green.

Off the tee on par-4 and par-5 holes she aims well away from trouble. "Usually the trouble on a drive is on one side or the other," Mrs. Rankin points out. "Driving into trouble almost automatically costs you at least one stroke, so play extra safe off the tee."

On her approach shots, on the other hand, she wants to put the ball in position for birdie putts. "I like to aim at the pin unless there's a compelling reason not to," she says. If the pin is closely guarded by dangerous hazards, of course, she advises caution.

A good game plan: play it safe off the tee and go for the pin on your approach.

KNOW YOUR LIMITS AND ACCEPT THEM

The best golf lesson Tom Watson ever got came from the late Leland (Duke) Gibson, a teaching pro in Kansas City, Kansas. Gibson told Watson to play the shot he was sure he could bring off, always.

Said Gibson: "Know what your limitations are, and understand what you can and can't do. Never try a shot you are not capable of or haven't practiced."

Gibson was counseling Watson to know when to take a risk and when to play safe. Watson points to the example of a little pop wedge shot over a hazard to a tight pin position. Do you gamble on getting the ball close with a tricky finesse shot, or do you simply put the ball on the green? To make a good decision, you have to know how well you play the finesse shot generally and how sharp your touch is on any particular day.

When in doubt, his old teacher stressed to Watson, take no chances.

Tom Watson

AVOID HORROR HOLES

Lou Graham's approach to professional golf is simple, conservative—and successful. His game plan from round to round never varies; play safely and shoot for 18 straight pars. The birdies, he reasons, will take care of themselves. For weekend players, the idea might be to play for 18 bogeys and let the pars take care of themselves, but the thrust is the same . . . avoid risky shots and play within your capabilities.

On the tee, Lou aims for the fat part of the fairway. On approach shots, he aims for the center of the green—rarely for the pin, which tends to be tucked near trouble.

Essentially, Graham wants to avoid the horrid hole that can ruin a round. That's smart golf for every level of play.

USE WARM-UP TO DETECT DAY'S FLIGHT PATTERN

By warming up before he tees off, the smart golfer isn't just loosening his muscles. He's studying the flight pattern of his shots to tell how he's hitting them that particular day.

Even the finest golfers swing a little differently and get varied results from one day to the next, because machines they're not. Doug Ford, the former Masters champion, once said: "You'll never wake up and hit the ball the same way you did the day before, so allow for it."

Toward the end of your warm-up, hit a minimum of 10 balls with a full swing. If you find yourself hooking your practice shots, assume you're going to hook during your round—even if you've been slicing for the last three weeks.

Play for the hook and keep the ball in the fairway and on the green. Never mind if your shots aren't picture perfect—you're putting together a score, not a photograph album. Use your warm-up to tell how your shots are bending—and make allowances when you go on the course.

SLOW DOWN BEFORE YOUR ROUND

World golfer Gary Player prepares for a round by eating slower, talking slower, walking slower—doing everything slower. He doesn't play slowly, but he takes his time preparing to play.

Golf is a game you cannot rush; you must play with composure. The average player has to fit a round of golf in amid many other activities. He'll hurry from home or office to the course, and he'll still be rushed when he gets on the first tee. He's apt to start poorly and go on to a discouraging round. He would do much better if he forced himself to slow down getting to the course, allowed time to stop at the practice range and hit a few balls, then moved—unhurried—to the first tee.

His chances of making a relaxed swing and getting off to the start of something good are ever so much greater.

Gary Player makes a conscious effort to slow down his entire life style before he plays. You can improve your game simply by slowing down in the hour or so before a round.

Gary Player

MAKE MODEST BETS TO COMPETE BETTER

Frank Beard risks the wrath of American motherhood when he suggests that junior golfers should bet their pocket money on the golf course. But he can make a good case for betting in golf at any age.

Beard reasons that you don't concentrate well on a golf course unless something is at stake. He contends that playing for 50 cents when he was 12 taught him to cope with the pressures of playing for $50,000 today. A bad shot hurt, and he'd find out what caused it so it didn't happen again. Now he wouldn't play a practice round without a bet. He wouldn't take it seriously enough. Most of the tour pros are the same way.

Beard doesn't mean we should bet beyond our means. He is saying that a modest wager can inspire us to learn new ways to score—to compete more intently.

Naturally you want to beware of the hustler who tries to get you in over your head or distract you. Decline last-second side bets and presses unless you're very steady under pressure.

TAKE TIME ON FIRST TEE

Jack Nicklaus considers the opening drive the most crucial shot of the day because it sets the tone for everything that follows. The great nemesis, on the first tee in the U.S. Open or the down-home closed, is tension. Nicklaus relieves it through de-lib-er-a-tion.

Even a player of his caliber is prone to hurry and get the first shot over with quickly. So he's extra deliberate in every thing he does on the first tee. In planning the shot, in setting up to the ball, in starting his swing, Jack makes sure he's ready before he hits the ball, and he swings with only about 85 percent of his power.

I'm reminded of the legendary Walter Hagen, who went to the first tee with one simple goal in mind: to get the ball airborne. Naturally, he wanted to hit it straight and far, but all he tried to do with his opening drive was get it up in the air.

Bill Rogers

SEPARATE PLAY THOUGHTS FROM PRACTICE THOUGHTS

British Open and World Series winner Bill Rogers thinks there's a time and a place for worrying about swing mechanics; the time is before or after a round and the place is the practice tee.

When you're on the course, you should play the game, not try to make perfect swings. Formulate a game plan for each hole and then visualize each shot in your mind as you prepare to hit it. Never mind the position of your right elbow at the top of your left hip at impact. Those are mechanical thoughts that belong on the practice tee, where you develop a better swing. On the course you develop lower scores, and you do that by using play thoughts. Swing technique is important, but if you work on it during a round, you probably will overcontrol the club and lose your freedom of motion.

As Bill Rogers puts it, learn to distinguish between your practice thoughts and your play thoughts, and leave your practice thoughts on the practice tee.

TACTICS ON THE COURSE

USE YOUR IMAGINATION IN TIGHT SPOTS

One recent summer Lon Hinkle stole the show at the U.S. Open in Toledo by playing the eighth hole from the 17th fairway, making the long par-5 reachable in two shots. Tournament officials planted a tree—"the Hinkle tree"— near the tee to discourage him, but it didn't.

Shortly after, in the World Series, the good-humored Hinkle once more was inventive. Under a tree after his second shot on the 600-yard 16th at Firestone Country Club, with a pond between his ball and the green, he appeared to have no shot. But he cleverly improvised— and skipped the ball off the water onto the green. On purpose. Hinkle had done it again.

Lon really isn't that much more imaginative than a lot of other pros; he just happened to be in a couple of conspicuous places at a couple of conspicuous times. Good golfers often use their imaginations to find a better way, while weekend players seldom will. Imagination can be the best weapon you have on the golf course—use it.

AIM BETWEEN TROUBLE SPOTS OFF THE TEE

When it comes to driving accuracy, young Mike Reid is golf's real straight arrow. Reid drove it in the fairway 80 percent of the time to lead the first tour accuracy statistics, and lest you think direction is less important than distance, consider that the 15 straightest drivers averaged $135,000 in winnings to the 15 longest drivers' $65,000.

Reid thinks most golfers are overly tense on the tee, because they try too hard to hit a precise spot in the fairway. His theory is to forget aiming at a spot and simply aim between the trouble . . . bunkers, rough, whatever. He recalls the words of Dodger pitching great Sandy Koufax: "You never aim a pitch—you just throw it."

To put the ball between the trouble, Reid curves it from left to right, his natural shot shape, aiming down the left side. Most of us hit the ball in a fairly predictable pattern, and should allow for it off the tee.

Then all you have to do, in the view of straight arrow Mike Reid, is aim between the trouble, not at a spot.

Raymond Floyd

AIM LEFT
AND LET 'ER FADE

Raymond Floyd is one of the many tour pros who never tries to hit a golf ball straight. He prefers to fade it from left to right, and contends the average player should do the same.

By fading the ball consistently, Floyd has more fairway or green to hit to. Here's his reasoning. If he tries to hit the ball straight down the center, he has only half the fairway to work with, he can miss the shot either left or right. But if he aims down the left edge of the fairway and fades the ball, he opens up the entire fairway. With his normal fade, he's in the left side of the fairway. If he fades it a little too much, he's in the center. If his fade turns into a slice—the worst that should happen—he's still in the fairway to the right.

Most golfers slice, and Floyd's advice to them is to aim left and allow for the curvature. The next stage of development would be to refine the slice into a Floydian Fade.

LEARN TO JUDGE DISTANCE BY BETTER PREPARATION

Weekend golfers lose strokes and confidence because they misjudge the distance on approach shots.

Here are three ways to judge distance more accurately.

1. Determine how far you hit each club. Knowing your target is 175 yards away won't help, if you have no idea whether you hit a 5-iron or a 5-wood from that distance. Take an hour or two on the driving range to learn your average distance with each club.

2. If you play most of your golf on one course, work out the yardage to the green from obvious landmarks on par-4 and par-5 holes. If it's 140 yards from the only tree near the 14th fairway to the green, you should know that.

3. Bear in mind that the location of the cup can make a difference of two and three clubs on today's big greens. A green a hundred feet deep could call for a 6-iron when the cup is in front and a 4-iron when it's in back. Consider the location of the cup before you choose a club.

WHEN TO USE MORE CLUB THAN NORMAL

Tom Watson claims underclubbing is the most prevalent tactical error in the game. Watson makes it a point to use more club than normal in these four situations:

1. When the air is damp. His normal 7-iron distance is 155-160 yards, but in wet, heavy air it's cut to 150 or less.

2. Playing into a strong headwind. Most golfers take one more club into the wind, but that may not be enough. If the wind is blowing harder than 10 miles an hour, Watson will go down at least two clubs . . . and many times four or five.

3. From an uphill lie. An uphill lie in effect adds loft to the club, so that a 6-iron shot will fly more like a 7-iron, or even an 8- or 9-iron if the slope is steep.

4. Shooting to an elevated green. The ball will land sooner on a raised green, and the higher the green is situated, the more club you need.

Arnold Palmer

TACTICS ON THE COURSE

'CHARGE' WITH PLENTY OF CLUB

Arnold Palmer's name is synonymous with exciting, aggressive golf, but are you ready for a surprise? The real reason for his success as a dramatic, come-from-behind charger is his cautious club selection, and that's something we all can learn from. Palmer makes sure he has enough club to carry the ball to the hole with a normal swing. Arnie doesn't care if his playing partners are using two clubs less than he is. He appreciates that picking a club isn't a masculinity contest, and so should we.

The most common mistake he sees amateurs make is not taking enough club for a shot into the green. A 14-handicapper may have hit a perfect 7-iron 150 yards three years ago, and ever since he's figured he's going to hit it that way every time. No chance, even if you're Arnold Daniel Palmer.

"A pro might hit only two or three shots a round he's truly proud of," Palmer points out. "But he gets the ball on the green consistently because he has plenty of club in his hands."

That's the way you charge, Arnold Palmer style.

TRY 3 KEYS PLAYING PAR-3'S

Many weekend golfers lose more strokes to par on little par-3 holes than on long par-4's and 5's. Playing par-3 golf holes, the emphasis should be on tactics rather than power. First, club selection is crucial. Most weekend golfers don't hit enough club on par-3's. Maybe they don't want to hit less club than their playing partners, or they don't notice that the green is elevated, or they don't appreciate that the trouble on modern courses is in front of the green. A good rule of thumb is to take one more club than you think you need and swing smoothly.

Second, always tee the ball on a par-3. The average golfer invariably makes better contact with the ball if it's teed. Tee the ball just above the grass and hit down and through. Try to break the tee on a par-3.

Third, par-3's usually have small greens guarded by menacing hazards. Play the percentages and shoot for the fat part of the green. Your chances of two-putting for a par will be good from anywhere on a small green.

To sharpen your play on par-3's, take one more club, tee the ball every time, and shoot for the fat part of the green.

Tom Weiskopf

IN MATCH PLAY, POUR ON PRESSURE RIGHT FROM THE START

Joanne Carner is one of the greatest competitors at match play in the history of women's and men's golf alike. Her thoughts on match-play tactics are revealing.

Joanne contends that most matches are won in the first few holes—that the player who takes the early lead probably will keep it. So her first priority is to concentrate fully at the outset of a match and get off to a good start. Then the pressure is on the opponent, who usually tries too hard to make birdies and instead makes costly mistakes.

Once Carner holds the upper hand, she watches her opponent closely for signs of emotional weakening. When she sees them, she closes in for a ladylike but ruthless kill. "When your opponent is shaky," says Carner, "that's the time to stomp. Show no mercy—take no prisoners. Finish it off with your best shots."

Joanne Carner has won dozens of big matches over the years using that clearly delineated strategy, and she commends it to weekend players. Concentrate on getting away to a fast start so the pressure is on your opponent, and when the opponent shows signs of shakiness—stomp!

Joanne Carner

BETTER-BALL POINTERS

In Ryder Cup golf, the pros try to keep pressure off their partners in four-ball matches. The straighter driver tees off first, even though he may be a shorter hitter. That way the team is virtually assured of having a ball in the fairway, and the second player has the option of taking a chance on a big drive.

The pros don't gamble as much as you might think in better-ball matches, though. They contend that the percentage way to make pars and birdies is to keep both balls in play.

When they compare notes on yardages, club selection and reading greens, the pros are wary of confusing each other with too much input.

The pros go out of their way to encourage their partners and build their confidence. The worst thing you can do is get down on your partner.

It's sharp better-ball strategy to let the straight driver tee off first, to avoid taking risky chances, and to encourage your partner—even if you feel like making him walk home.

PLAY SAFE, ESPECIALLY IN THE SPRING

Early in the season is no time to try to be a hero on the golf course. Play safe until you gain confidence in your game. Ease into each new season with conservative strategy.

Example: Drive with a 3-wood or even an iron and leave your driver in the bag for a few rounds, being sure you put the ball in play off the tee.

Example: If you have a choice, don't attempt to carry any hazard unless you can make it easily with an iron. When in doubt about getting over a big water hazard, lay up or play around it.

Example: On your approach shots, hit for the center of the green. Don't aim at the flagstick if there's trouble anywhere near it. You still always have a good chance to get down in two putts.

In the spring, play safe until your game rounds into shape.

6.
MENTAL PLOYS

CURE FIRST-TEE JITTERS IN 15 SECONDS

Teeing off on the first hole in front of waiting foursomes can be as traumatic as playing "Hamlet" before a royal audience, particularly if you haven't hit any practice balls.

How do you cope with nervousness and anxiety on the golf course? Dr. David Morley, a psychiatrist, who happens to be crazy about golf, has some advice he has found helpful.

Morley says the first step is to acknowledge your anxiety. Appreciate that it's a real problem that must be dealt with.

"The second step," Dr. Morley says, "is to use your imagination to control the anxiety.

"Think of your body as a receptacle filled with a fluid that is anxiety, or nervousness," he urges. "Let the fluid drain out of your body, starting at the top of your head and moving down to the end of your toes."

Morley says the technique takes only about 15 seconds once you get used to it, and will produce impressive results. It has been used in hypnosis work all over the world for years to reduce tension.

The next time anxiety attacks you on the first tee, imagine the anxiety is a fluid that fills your body, and let it drain out from head to toe.

BECOME A TOUGHER COMPETITOR

His friends call pro golfer Hale Irwin "Fierce" for his intense competitiveness. I asked Irwin to give us weekend players three thoughts on being more competitive, and here's what he came up with.

First, make every shot the critical one. Irwin isolates each shot in a round of golf and treats it as a separate challenge, forgetting what happened on previous holes or what lies ahead.

Second, says Irwin, consider difficult conditions an advantage. He prefers playing in the wind or rain, or on a difficult course, because he knows other players will get discouraged.

Third, keep moving forward. If you get a big lead, try to make it bigger. Don't allow yourself to coast, because once you lose your momentum, says Irwin, it's like sliding on ice—you can't stop.

Andy Bean

PLAY IN PRESENT TENSE

Your concentration in golf should always be on the shot you're playing and not on how your overall score is progressing. The key is to play in the present tense at all times, mentally blocking out what's already happened or what future holes hold in store.

Average players have a dangerous tendency to start projecting the total score for a round with several holes still to play, especially if they're playing better than usual. For example, they may think to themselves they have only to bogey the last three holes to break 90 for the first time. Distracted, they may not break a hundred.

On a higher level, the best tour pros can fall into the same trap. Birdie strings end when the pros stop playing one shot at a time and start wondering how long they can keep the hot streak going.

To concentrate better, stay in the present tense and give your full attention to each shot as it presents itself, letting your final score take care of itself. It will come out lower that way.

DRAW THE CURTAIN OF CONCENTRATION

Ben Hogan was the epitome of concentration in golf. He all but stared the ball into the hole. Hogan disciplined himself to focus intently on his round from the time he changed into his spikes in the locker room until he putted out on the 18th green. If he saw his wife on the course he didn't recognize her.

You and I aren't motivated to concentrate thoroughly for five hours, or conditioned to do it. We'd exhaust ourselves with the effort.

A more realistic goal is to concentrate fully for 30 seconds before each shot. Try using an image of a stage curtain coming down in your head half a minute before a shot. That's your curtain of concentration. In 30 seconds you have plenty of time to size up the shot, decide how to hit it and visualize a happy result.

Once the shot is struck, the curtain comes up. Between shots, enjoy the scenery and the conversation with your group. Then, 30 seconds before your next shot, drop the curtain of concentration again.

Ben Hogan

TAKE THE TRAUMA OUT OF SHORT TROUBLE SHOTS

Some of the little shots in golf can be the most intimidating. Take the short pitch over a deep bunker or water hazard with the pin cut close to the near edge of the green. Most of us would rather fight a bear with a bag towel than face this little number with a $1 nassau at stake.

But it doesn't have to be so traumatic. To start with, mentally block out the hazard. Look past it and concentrate on your target, visualizing the shot that will get the ball there. Imagine how you would play the shot if the sand or water didn't exist, because that's all you have to do. Trust in a lofted iron club to do the job without any special assistance from you. You'll probably want to pick a wedge. Don't try to help the club get the ball over the trouble by "scooping" at the shot. You hit down on the ball to make it go up (nobody ever said golf wasn't a game of opposites).

You can almost guarantee a solid downward hit by choking down on the grip, shortening your backswing and keeping more weight on your left side throughout the stroke.

Then just be sure you accelerate the clubhead into the ball. Think of an airplane taking off. It had better be accelerating, and the same is true of the clubhead on a short pitch over trouble.

Jerry Pate

Bobby Jones

ONE THOUGHT'S ENOUGH

The legendary Bobby Jones once said that when he was playing golf well he thought of only one thing while making a shot. And when he was playing really well, he thought of nothing at all!

The average player addresses the ball running through a 50-point checklist . . . everything from "keep the left arm straight" to "finish high." He becomes a victim of that dread disease, "paralysis by analysis."

Breaking down your swing mechanically is fine—on the practice range. On the golf course it's ruinous. Hopefully you've ingrained good mechanics through intelligent practice. If you haven't, it's too late now.

Many leading players think solely of the target. They visualize the shot they need to get the ball there, then let the subconscious produce the correct swing. If you've been letting a parade of mechanical thoughts march through your head, try thinking only of the target . . . and Bobby Jones.

KEEP YOUR EMOTIONS UNDER CONTROL

Tension is a major menace of the weekend golfer. It can cause more bad shots than a shout on your backswing. How do you beat tension?

Begin by understanding that a certain amount of it is essential to doing anything well, whether it's playing golf or blowing glass. If you aren't nervous, you aren't "up" for an activity . . . you won't be alert or strong. Any pro star will tell you emphatically that the day he walks onto the first tee and doesn't get butterflies in his stomach is the day he should stay in bed. The more important the tournament, the more restive the butterflies. Fuzzy Zoeller says he got nervous the year he won the Masters just driving through the front gate of the grounds.

The trick is to keep your tension in context and under control.

Mentally relax. As Dave Marr tells his uptight pro-am partners, there's no awful shot you can show him that he hasn't seen before, including a clean miss. Remind yourself that millions of Chinese couldn't care less where your shot goes.

Then relax your grip. If you're overly nervous, you probably have a stranglehold on the club that is tensing your body right down to your toes. Relaxing your grip pressure can free up your entire swing. Now you're ready to let tension work for you instead of against you.

KEEP A 'LITTLE BLACK BOOK'

The best investment you can make in your golf game might not be an expensive set of new clubs or even a series of lessons. It might be a 35-cent spiral notepad.

Once you are convinced that the only way you can lower your handicap is by practicing, and I hope you are, you should practice those areas of your game that consistently let you down.

It's hard to know what to practice without keeping at least a cursory chart on your play. I suggest you enter in a little black book after each round a few key statistics such as: the number of fairways you hit off the tee, the number of greens you hit in regulation figures, the number of times you chipped to within one-putt distance. Also the number of times you got out of green-side bunkers to within one-putt distance, and the number of times you got down in two putts from farther away than 15 feet.

Then if you find, for example, that your long putts are failing you, spend more practice time on long putts. Keep track of your play—and cut your scores—by making notes after each round.

Beth Daniel

PLAY ALL SHOTS LIKE TROUBLE SHOTS

Concentration, in golf or anything else, means total involvement in your task. It's a mental skill that takes practice to develop, just like a physical skill.

To sharpen your concentration, start on the practice green, two feet from the hole, sinking mini-putts. Then move back a few feet, then a few feet more. At each stage set a goal—six out of eight, or 10 out of 15.

Move off the green and apply this approach to all the clubs in your bag up through the driver. Your concentration will be more keenly focused.

On the course most golfers use too much physical effort and not enough mental effort. Address the ball with a positive swing key in mind—"keep your grip pressure light," for instance. This induces concentration.

Staying on an even emotional keel will help you keep your concentration. Don't become despondent over a bad hole, or too excited over a good one.

Your concentration usually is best on a trouble shot, when you apply your powers fully. If you can start taking the routine shots that seriously, you're on your way to good concentration.

GAMESMANSHIP CAN BE FAIR

One golfer can gain an advantage over another by using psychological ploys, particularly in match play. That's called gamesmanship, and the gambits range from the outrageously unfair to the acceptably strategic. Let me give you a couple of subtle tactics that can put you in control of a match without compromising the code of the game.

Observe your opponent on the first few holes and determine whether he likes to play slowly or quickly. Then give him every chance to lose his natural rhythm. If he's a slow player, move briskly to speed him up.

Gamesmanship really gets going on the greens. Concede your opponent short putts on the early holes, to keep him from building his confidence and getting a grasp of the greens. Then later, when he has a crucial short putt with some break in it, make him putt it. Walter Hagen, the past master of match play, used this one to unnerve many opponents.

Gamesmanship—practiced in the proper way—can and should be a legitimate part of your strategy.

7.
IMPROVEMENT
POINTERS

3 SMART WAYS TO PRACTICE

Ben Hogan is probably the greatest practicer in the history of golf, if not all sport. In his prime he made practice an eight-hour duty, seven days a week—working tirelessly on every shot he could imagine.

We don't have to be as diligent as Hogan, but it's essential to practice intelligently if you hope to improve. Here are three practice hints to help you play better.

1. Give every shot your full attention. Don't rush just because you paid for a big bucket of range balls. Set the bucket behind you, so you have to go through your setup procedure on each shot.

2. Hit every shot to a specific target, for both direction and distance. Make believe you are playing a certain hole at your home course and include trouble shots.

3. Practice following a round. Fifteen minutes of work after you play, when your bad shots are fresh in mind, can be more valuable than 15 hours of pre-round practice.

PRACTICE BRIEFLY BUT REGULARLY

It's one thing to be told you have to practice to play better. It's quite another to find the time. Professional golfers enjoy the luxury of practicing literally hours every day. We don't. Yet we would improve dramatically if we could find time to practice a mere 30 minutes three times a week.

What about on your lunch hour or after work?

You're better off hitting 40 or 50 balls three times a week than belting out three large buckets, one after another. About all you do in a marathon practice session is wear yourself out and develop award-winning blisters.

Avoid the tendency to rush because you have only 30 minutes. Put the balls down behind you, so you have to take time between shots. Start with your shorter clubs and save the driver until last, hitting every shot at a target and swinging every club with the same tempo.

Practice meaningfully for 30 minutes three times a week, after work or on your lunch hour, and you'll soon see your scores coming down.

Jack Nicklaus

CURE SLUMP WITH A SHORT IRON AND SHAG BAG

You are allowed 14 clubs in your bag, and the temptation is strong to give every one of them a workout when you go to the range.

The average golfer would be better off practicing with one club than with all 14: a short iron. It's much easier to develop a grooved swing, especially early in the season.

Too many of us take the name "driving range" literally. We spend the bulk of our practice time bashing out driver shots and trying to hit the 250 sign. That makes it hard to ingrain a sound, well-paced swing.

With a shorter club, you should feel no urge to strain for distance. (If you need more distance, all you have to do is take a longer iron.) Your swing arc is shorter, affording added control over the club.

In practice, concentrate on making smooth, rhythmic swings, with a short club. Working with a short iron is extra valuable when your game falls off.

Old Dutch Harrison used to say that hitting a bucket of balls with a 9-iron is the best cure for a slump. It also can be the best way to duck one.

USE SPOT-AIMING TO SHARPEN ALIGNMENT

Dr. Gil Morgan is often called a "non-practicing optometrist" on the TPA pro tour. That's not so. His training in optometry helps him every time he plays golf.

Gil practices and preaches the importance of correct optics in golf, mainly through spot-aiming. The theory is that it's easier to aim at a target six feet away than one six hundred feet away.

Morgan makes his shots easier to line up by bringing his target closer. Bowlers are familiar with spot-aiming. They roll the ball over a close-in painted spot on the alley and don't worry about the distant pins. Spot-aiming in golf works the same way.

First, stand behind the ball and sight down the line to your target. Next pick a spot a few feet in front of the ball on your target line. It can be a divot mark or a patch of light grass or a leaf.

Now move into your stance. Aim the clubface first, line up to hit the ball over the intermediate spot and start the ball out over it.

TRY FEET-TOGETHER DRILL TO RESTORE BALANCED SWING

A proven golf practice drill is to swing with your feet together. You can do it in your garage or basement on a rainy day.

Start with a short iron and your feet together. If you're on the range, put the ball on a tee. Swing slowly at first and gradually increase your pace as you gain a better sense of balance. You'll be surprised, by the way, how far you can hit the ball with your feet together.

The feet-together exercise makes you turn your shoulders and hips rather than sway from side to side, your arms swinging freely up and down. If you sway with your feet together, you lose your balance.

As you begin to master the drill, widen your stance and work up to longer clubs—but remember how you felt when you swung with your feet together. If you lose that feel, go back to practice-swinging with your feet together. You'll get your tempo together too.

PULL RIGHT SHOULDER BACK TO STRAIGHTEN SLICE

It is reliably estimated that nine out of ten golfers are afflicted with a slice, that dismaying shot that careens weakly from left to right for a righthander.

The usual reaction to a slice on the part of its victim makes matters worse. In an effort to keep the ball away from the right side of the course, the righthanded slicer opens his shoulders—aligns them more to the left. Now the backswing turn is blocked, the outside-in path of the downswing that causes a slice is exaggerated—and the ball bends still farther right.

Look to the position of your right shoulder at address to straighten out a slice. Pull your right shoulder back until your shoulders are slightly 'closed,' or aligned a bit to the right of your target. Now you can make a stronger, inside-out downswing. The right shoulder works 'down and under' through the hitting area instead of 'out and around.'

It sounds contradictory, but in a game of seeming contradictions, it works.

IMPROVEMENT POINTERS

SWING WITHOUT SWAY TO END FAT SHOTS

A leading cause of fat shots in golf is swaying off the ball on your backswing—letting your weight shift too far to your right if you're a right-hander.

Think of the golf swing as being basically a circle drawn by the movement of the clubhead. The radius is a line formed by your left arm and the club shaft. The center of the circle is your head. In a good swing, the circle touches the ground at one point—the ball. If you sway on your backswing, the entire circle shifts. On the downswing the club will hit behind the ball unless you make a well-timed sway back to the left, and you won't do that consistently.

To prevent swaying, flex your right knee slightly and cock it toward your left knee at address. Then on the backswing don't let your weight move farther right than the inside of your right foot. Practicing with an old-fashioned door stop under the outside of the right foot has been known to induce the feeling of a controlled weight shift.

PUT COMPETITIVE ZEAL IN YOUR PRACTICE

Practice is essential if you want to improve, but practice doesn't have to be tedious. The main reason golfers find practice boring is there's no immediate reward. The secret is to introduce an element of competition.

Making your practice competitive will improve your concentration and your scores. Not only that, your sessions with the shag bag will be a lot more enjoyable.

For starters, take to the putting clock and place 25 balls three feet from the cup. Allow yourself 27 strokes to "win" this little contest.

Then move the balls farther from the cup and adjust your scoring standards. Follow the same procedure for chip shots. Out of the sand, try to get two-thirds of your shots on the green. Work your way up to full drives, always competing against yourself.

You can adjust your criteria in all cases to fit your handicap level. But the overriding point is to make your practice competitive.

Isao Aoki

PRACTICE PUTTING WITHOUT A BACKSTROKE

There are two major causes of poor putting: failure to accelerate the putter into the ball, and failure to meet the ball with the putterface square to the target.

An easy golf practice drill can help you accelerate the putter through the ball with a square face.

Put a dozen balls down in a circle around the hole—five or six feet away. By forcing yourself to move for each putt, you ensure that you line up with care. Now, address each ball and, without using a backswing, try to push it into the cup.

Repeat—do not use a backswing. Place the putter directly behind the ball and stroke through it from there. You will gain a new feeling for the putter accelerating through the ball.

Keep the blade square to your target. To check it, hold your finish position and see if the face of the putter is looking at the hole. Putting without a backswing and checking the face for squareness results in more-solid contact and more accuracy.

PRACTICE LONG AND SHORT PUTTS

When weekend golfers practice putting, they commonly work on 15-footers. They may be wasting their time.

The average golfer faces a lot of 35-foot putts after he hits a long shot barely onto the green. And he faces a lot of five-footers after he misses the green and chips on. But he doesn't see a lot of 15-foot putts. So why practice them?

It makes sense to practice the putts you can make and the putts you will get frequently. Practice the five-footers. A 90 to 100 shooter is liable to miss five or 10 of these putts a round, largely because he seldom practices them. Making five-footers is a quick way to cut your scores. Line them up carefully and make a firm stroke.

You can work on short putts indoors if the weather fails you. Practice the five-foot putt until it's an old friend, because you'll face it frequently. Let the 15-footers take care of themselves.

EXTEND YOUR SEASON

I know a weekend golfer who always ends his season on Labor Day. It's a shame, for two reasons. First, the fall can be the best time of year for golf, in terms of both weather and scenery, and winter isn't necessarily unplayable. Second, these early hibernators are missing a good chance to improve their games.

Most weekend golfers are playing better by the end of the summer, and they figure they can lay off for several months, then pick up next spring where they left off. But when spring comes, they're back where they started.

If you decide to keep playing through the off-season you may be amazed how many playable golfing days there are. The weather doesn't have to be perfect. If the temperature's above 40 and the ground's firm you can enjoy the game. An added benefit is faster play on less crowded courses.

USE INDOOR LESSONS TO GET BACK TO BASICS

A growing legion of leading golf teachers contends that the average player can learn more taking lessons indoors than outdoors—for two good reasons.

Reason No. 1 is that indoors you are swing-oriented instead of shot-oriented. You can think about mechanics and tempo rather than distance and direction.

The second good reason is that indoors there are fewer distractions, making it easier to pay attention to the instructor. You can concentrate on the message and forget the milieu.

Taking lessons indoors in the off-season is an especially good way to "get back to basics" before you challenge the course and the elements—a review of fundamentals can lay the foundation for a good year.

Some teaching pros in and around major cities have set up elaborate indoor facilities, complete with driving nets and computerized swing-check machines, so you can sharpen your game on your lunch hour. Come spring, you'll be glad you did.

PAMPER YOUR CLUBS

How well are you taking care of your clubs? Keeping them in good shape can help you play better—and help the clubs last longer.

Many weekend golfers throw their clubs in the trunk of the car at the start of the season and leave them there when they're not playing. That's about the worst thing you can do. Your wood heads can dry out and crack, or take on moisture and expand. Shafts can warp, grips deteriorate, irons get nicked and scarred.

Your woods should be protected with head covers—even during a round. Wet covers should be removed immediately after you play and the heads toweled off. Shafts should be wiped clean to prevent rusting. Soak the heads of your irons in warm soapy water or scour them with a detergent pad.

Don't forget the grips, which affect your hold on the club and get slick with use. Clean them with soap and water or a detergent pad, and if they're still slippery use sandpaper to roughen them.

Pampering your golf clubs will pay off—in playability and in money saved, because they last longer.

27/8/82
2/41 YCB
54.4° Lett